Walking Alone

~ A Pilgrim's Guide to the
Inner Journey ~

Cover Photo: Mony Dojeiji and Alberto Agraso
Cover Design: Alberto Agraso
Original Illustrations: Alberto Agraso

Walking for Peace Publishing
2017

First Edition

Walking Alone

~ A Pilgrim's Guide to the
Inner Journey ~

Mony Dojeiji

Mony Dojeiji

DEDICATION
To those who journey by themselves:
you never walk alone.

CONTENTS

ACKNOWLEDGMENTS

My thanks, as always, to my pilgrim partner in life Alberto Agraso for your wisdom, love and support. *Te quiero.*

INTRODUCTION

INTRODUCTION

Information abounds to help the pilgrim prepare for the physical aspects of their pilgrimage – what to wear, how to get there, what to carry – but little to no attention is paid to the mental, emotional and spiritual elements that make the Camino, or any other sacred walk, a pilgrimage rather than a hike.

I walked my first Camino alone in 2001, long before the phenomenon that it has become today. There was only one guidebook in English and no information online. I showed up without preparing or training, and carrying way too much weight in my backpack. I quickly learned what was essential and what was frivolous.

My body surprised me with its adaptability. I was generally fit, but unprepared for walking as a pilgrim, and not merely as a walker rushing to get to her destination. Blisters were my main companion – and teacher – on the Camino. From them, I would learn to slow down and walk in the unhurried manner of the pilgrim.

Although I was prepared for physical discomfort, no one warned me about the emotional rollercoaster I would be riding – from jubilation to dejection – often in the same day. No one prepared me to deal with thoughts that would both betray and empower me. No one spoke about facing fears and personal demons, especially when walking alone. And certainly no one mentioned the shift in consciousness and the opening to Spirit that would take place during pilgrimage.

On my first Camino, I would learn the importance of making peace with my fears, of trusting the path that was leading me to my destination and, above all, of opening my heart to the miracles and magic that had always been there. These would set the foundation for my later walking 5000 kilometers (3500 miles) from Rome to Jerusalem, a pilgrimage more ancient than Santiago but with no marked path, trails, yellow arrows, albergues or infrastructure of any kind to support the pilgrim in their journey. Had the Camino not prepared me emotionally, mentally and spiritually for pilgrimage, I never would have been able to make it to Jerusalem.

That was its greatest gift to me.

What I now believe is that pilgrimage isn't merely the outer act of walking towards a sacred destination, be it Santiago de Compostela or some other holy site. The outer destination gives me the goal. It holds the promise of secret knowledge and wisdom that I will somehow attain when I arrive there.

But the true temple, the true destination, is inner: a sacred place where all questions are answered and all that I need for my life's journey is provided.

It is to this place that I journey when I walk, and what makes the experiences along the way such powerful elixirs for that personal transformation to occur so that I may touch the light of the truly sacred within.

I would return twice more to the Camino, to walk sections of it, and deepen my practice of walking to a sacred inner location disguised as a walk to an outer temple.

Unlike physical preparations, there is no checklist to prepare you mentally, emotionally and spiritually. What I offer you are reflections based on my personal experiences and countless presentations I have given on how to prepare for the inner journey. It is my sincere hope that they serve you in your pilgrimage.

With this, as with any other material related to pilgrimage, I encourage you to take what makes sense to your heart and mind, and leave the rest behind. There is no "right way" to do a pilgrimage. It is a journey as unique as the pilgrim, and one that you must walk in a way that honors all your needs.

In some chapters, you will find questions and exercises intended to help you prepare for the mental, emotional and spiritual aspects of your pilgrimage. I also share ideas on how to put your preparations into practice during your pilgrimage, and in your everyday life.

In fact, I believe that your life is your pilgrimage, and that you don't need to go to a sacred site to be a pilgrim. You already are one. These exercises are a foundation for being a pilgrim in life, on or off a pilgrimage path. It may be an interesting exercise for you to answer these questions not only before you leave, but after you come back, to see how your perspectives have changed.

Finally, you will hear the word "love" more often in this book than in any other speaking about pilgrimage because, to me, it is the foundation of being able to walk alone. Pilgrimage is an expression of self-love and honors what is sacred in our lives. It offers the space for us to experience firsthand the Love that all of creation feels for us.

Thank you for joining me on this journey. To learn more about my walk, I invite you to visit my website http://walkingforpeace.com, where you will find maps, photos, stories and an excerpt of my international award-winning book "Walking for Peace, an inner journey".

For those looking for more personalized guidance for their inner preparations, I can be contacted for private sessions at monydojeiji@walkingforpeace.com.

Buen (inner) camino!
~Mony

POWER OF PILGRIMAGE

2 POWER OF PILGRIMAGE

I love pilgrimage because it gets you out of your routine and places you firmly in the unknown. And it is in the unknown that we grow beyond all that defines us.

There is something incredibly powerful and ancient in putting one step in front of the other. Walk long enough, and the steps take on a life of their own, moving in a rhythm that is independent of thought. You may even reach a point where you don't even feel your body. Walking becomes a form of meditation, where your steps guide you deeper inwards to that sacred place within you.

The body is a magnificent instrument and the easiest aspect to train because it adapts to whatever you put it though. The work is to train your mind and heart to similarly adapt and expand.

Like the fabled Ithaka – the beautiful poem by C. Cavafy – pilgrimage gives you the destination. It gives you the dream to embark on the quest, but it's rarely about the destination. It sounds cliché, but it is truly about the journey, for it is on the journey that you:

◊ Ask – and begin to answer – the important questions of your life.

◊ Face your fears and make peace with your inner tormentors.

◊ Learn to trust yourself and know that all your needs will be provided for.

◊ Begin to understand your place in the universal order of things.

THAT is the journey I want to prepare you for!

When you are prepared to walk that journey towards self-knowing and self-mastery, then you can go on any quest, and you will have the tools you need to get to your destination – physical or spiritual.

STORY OF MY INNER JOURNEY

3 STORY OF MY INNER JOURNEY

It has taken me more than fifteen years to speak with confidence about what it really means to walk alone, and the shift that needed to happen within me so that I could do just that, on and off the pilgrimage path.

That shift did not happen overnight.

Three decades ago, I began my adult life as any other person. I pursued a B.Sc. and an MBA, and began my career in the corporate world, first as a Consultant at one of the Big 6 Consulting firms, and then in various business and marketing management roles at Microsoft's head offices in Canada and the U.S.

I lived what would be considered an ordinary life. I was married, lived in a comfortable house and paid my taxes. I had no aspirations beyond climbing the corporate ladder, moving to a bigger house, maybe having children one day; but nothing more.

When my husband left for another woman, my world collapsed. I couldn't understand why this was happening to me because I had done all the right things. I had played by society's rules and followed what I was told would make me successful, happy and fulfilled.

Why did I feel empty?

Why was I now all alone?

My search for answers led me to therapists and counselors, and although I understood psychologically and intellectually what had happened to me, my heart felt empty. I yearned for something more meaningful to fill an ache I couldn't explain. It was then that more spiritual texts of the time – including Deepak Chopra, Gary Zukov, James Redfield and Neale Donald Walsch – entered my life.

They challenged me to take responsibility for my life, and to move beyond the victim identity I had attached myself to. They opened my mind to a paradigm of the world I had never considered: that I am not alone in this vast Universe; that a great Love accompanies me; that I am an eternal being of light clothing itself in a body that allows it to play in this world; that my essence is Love, and that I come from this Love for the sole purpose of experimenting and growing in Love; and that ultimately, I am a much more powerful creator and child of Love than I dare to believe.

It all resonated so deeply; but how do you live this vision of yourself practically, in your day-to-day life?

How do you let go of the need to plan and control every aspect of your life, and simply flow?

How do you trust your non-physical senses and believe in what you can't see or touch?

How do you remain present, confident in the moment where you are, not thinking about the future, and allow the next step to reveal itself?

I didn't have the answers, but I was committed to the task of finding out, and becoming this kind of person. Held before me was the promise of a life filled with meaning and steadfast purpose, if I could be anchored in this new way of being. This, to me, was much more important than any salary or status I could receive.

It took me three years to work up the courage, but I eventually abandoned the corporate career that defined me, left the stock options that offered me security, and began my quest.

Traveling alone, and later pilgrimage, would provide me with the means to create this person and to put to the test all of the ideas and promises I had read about to see if they were true for me.

Living alone, going out alone, and finally traveling alone were the stepping stones. Of course I was afraid, but the journey was about making peace with those fears and going anyways.

In January of 2001, I bought a one-year open ticket,

starting in Egypt. The only organized activity was a cruise of the Nile. The rest, I was going to practice letting go of control and allowing my intuition and this Universal Love to guide me.

I made mistakes, over-trusting people, but quickly learned discernment. I learned that it was important to lead with the heart, but not completely dismiss the mind. The two must work in tandem and, in Egypt, I practiced doing just that.

After five months of traveling in Egypt and Europe alone, I was ready for pilgrimage. I arrived in St. Jean Pied du Port without planning or preparation, bought the only English guidebook available, and started walking the Camino (French Way) alone. The Camino would be the place where I would fully practice trusting the path, trusting my own inner yellow arrows – rather than the outer ones – for guidance, and trusting the Love that was walking with me and awakening deeply within me.

I walked, asking for clarity, to be shown the next steps in my life that would allow me to live with purpose and meaning.

I would receive that answer in the form of a conversation I would overhear among some pilgrims one day on the *Meseta*.

They spoke about three paths of personal initiation and transformation that each person is invited to walk on their journey of self-knowing.

The Camino to Santiago was the Way of the Sword, the place where you battle your personal demons and find your strength and courage, symbolized by the sword.

Walking to Rome, you walk the Way of the Heart and begin to understand the meaning of love, beyond the physical and into all its dimensions and aspects.

Walking to Jerusalem, you walk the Way of the Soul where you connect with your highest calling and understand how to use your life in the service of Love.

It was the Way of the Soul that inflamed my heart and

imagination, and I determined to walk it, starting in Rome, destination of the Way of the Heart.

It all seemed so clear and so easy…until I came off the Camino. In sharing this idea with family and friends, and then hearing the warnings and admonitions about all the dangers, the luster of my dream began to wear off. Ever so slowly, reason and logic won over what I knew in my heart to be my truth. The idea receded to the depths of memory.

Until 9/11.

Those events propelled me to action, awakening me from the stupor that fear had drawn me into. I decided I would walk the Way of the Soul from Rome to Jerusalem for peace, not because I had the answers for peace or was any poster child for it, but as my contribution to the voices of peace, unity and reconciliation.

In November of that same year 2001, I made my way to Vatican City, planning to walk alone; but a chance (or serendipitous) visit to a friend's home along the way changed everything.

I had met Alberto Agraso, a Spanish pilgrim, in Finisterre, a town whose name literally means "end of the world". We had both finished walking our own separate Caminos and, in that afternoon together, he had enthused about my idea of walking to Jerusalem. When we parted ways that same afternoon, wishing each other a *buen camino*, I never expected to see him again.

Imagine my shock at finding him at my friend's house!

He would feel the same calling as I did to embark on this Way of the Soul and to explore more deeply the many opportunities for spiritual growth it promised. While he prepared to leave his life behind, I traveled to Vatican City and began walking alone. Ten days later, he joined me. We would separate once more, this time for forty days in Croatia, with no way to contact one another. That time alone, however, would prove invaluable in cementing my confidence (and his) in walking alone.

Those experiences would firmly set me on the path of inner exploration, a journey which continues to this day.

For your reference, I include a map of the path we walked from Rome to Jerusalem. To see our daily route with kilometers walked and short stories, I invite you to visit our website http://walkingforpeace.com.

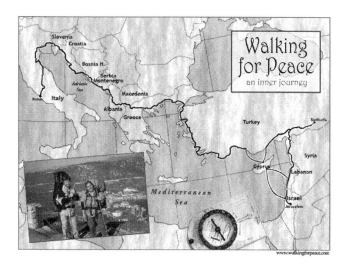

PREPARING THE MENTAL JOURNEY

4 PREPARING THE MENTAL JOURNEY

The mind is a powerful instrument and can be your greatest ally, or tormentor.

Understanding its workings and befriending it are keys in walking alone with confidence.

Make your Plans

For the mind to rest and be at peace, it must go through the planning and preparation for its unknown adventure ahead. It seeks to create order out of chaos and safety out of potential dangers. So be sure to do your research and learn as much as you can about your pilgrimage. It puts your mind at ease, and makes you feel prepared and under control.

There are some excellent online resources, including:

American Pilgrims on the Camino
http://www.americanpilgrims.org/
Canadian Company of Pilgrims
https://www.santiago.ca/
Australian Friends of the Camino
http://www.afotc.org/
Confraternity of Pilgrims to St. James
https://www.csj.org.uk/
Camino Forum
https://www.caminodesantiago.me/community/
Camino Adventures
https://www.caminoadventures.com/

Also be sure to look for the Pilgrim Associations in your city or country.

At the end of this book, I dedicate a chapter to international pilgrimages, and some considerations for you as you prepare to walk these often unstructured, unmarked and unorganized paths.

I will not dwell on the physical aspects of preparation because this information abounds.

What these sites may not tell you, however, is that no matter how much you plan, prepare and train, the first week of pilgrimage is always one of adaptation.

You're often walking six to eight hours a day, every day, always carrying your backpack. You may be faced with rain, wind, mud, snow, extreme heat or weather conditions unlike those in your home country. You're also in a foreign land whose culture differs from your own, often not understanding the language, eating new foods, sharing close quarters and facilities with complete strangers in various forms of undress and whose ideas of modesty are quite different from your own.

All these factors can add a layer of stress to some, or the thrill of discovery for others.

No matter where you are on this scale, give yourself permission to go slowly, and allow your physical body and all your senses to acclimatize to this new setting.

One of the keys to preventing injuries and allowing your body to adapt is to walk slowly, in the unhurried pace of the pilgrim, not the frantic rush of the walker. Pilgrimage is not a race, and if you find yourself in anxiety over where you will sleep that night, then I encourage you to book private accommodations in advance. This does not make you "less" of an authentic pilgrim. It frees you to focus on the inner journey that defines the pilgrim.

Another key is regular stretching. It is often overlooked and underestimated in the desire to build strength and stamina. They are, without a doubt, important elements of preparation, but keeping your muscles limber, supple, flexible will carry you the longer distances and make the physical journey more enjoyable. I highly encourage you to build that into your daily practice and preparations.

Above all else, relax. Your body will settle into the routine of pilgrimage, of waking up every day, putting on your backpack, walking your distance, and doing it all over again the next day. One step at a time, with great patience and love for the journey, will get you to your destination.

Ask yourself...

Have I done sufficient research into:
◊ Clothing and gear
◊ Testing and walking with all my gear
◊ Physical training regimen that includes strength, endurance and flexibility training; and that includes walking in adverse weather conditions and all kinds of terrain
◊ Joining a walking club or Camino group in my city
◊ Mobile and digital devices, and whether I will be carrying them
◊ Travel plans
◊ Health insurance
◊ Banking needs - advising my bank, and making sure I have a 4-digit pin
◊ Visa requirements (if any) for my country
◊ Advising my embassy of my travel plans
◊ Sharing my itinerary with those who support me

What aspects of my physical preparation am I most confident about?

What concerns do I still have about my physical readiness?

What flexibility exercises, in addition to my strength and endurance training, have I incorporated?

How can I address those concerns, if any?

What more can I do to put my mind at ease about my physical readiness?

Examine your Beliefs

We all walk with this invisible companion, one who will deeply influence your pilgrimage.

> What you believe will become your truth.

So, what thoughts dominate your mind? What do you accept to be true and unchanging? What do you believe without question? There is no right or wrong answer, but what you believe will become your truth, and you will experience it in your reality.

Let me share with you this tale of the traveler and the old man to illustrate this point.

At the gates of an ancient city deep in the desert sat a wise, old man. Travelers came and went, all under his gentle, watchful gaze.

One afternoon, a traveler arrived at the gates. The old man greeted him, and upon exchanging pleasantries, the traveler asked, "Tell me, old man, what kind of people live in this town? I'm thinking of moving and want to know more about this place."

"What kind of people live in the town where you come from?" Responded the man.

"Horrible!" Said the traveler. "You can't trust anyone. Thieves and pickpockets are everywhere. People have no regard for anyone except themselves. You have to keep a close eye on your possessions at all times. I can't tell you how much I'm looking forward to leaving that place! That's why I'm looking here. Please, my old friend, what is this town like?"

"I'm afraid it's exactly as the place you come from," the old man replied.

"Oh, thank you so much for letting me know," the traveler said. "You have saved me a great deal of trouble."

Days passed. The sun rose and set over the desert until, one fine afternoon, another traveler stopped at the doors of the town and greeted the old man.

"Tell me, old man, what kind of people live in this town? I'm thinking of moving and want to know more about this place."

"What kind of people live in the town you come from?" Asked the old man.

"Marvelous!" The traveler answered. "I can't tell you how fortunate I feel to know the people there. They are kind, generous, honest, always willing to lend a hand. I feel a welcome part of their community. It pains me to leave, but my work brings me to this place. Please, kind man, tell me, what is the character of this town and its people?"

"The people here are exactly as the ones from your town," the old man smiled in response.

The moral of the story is clear. It's not simply about the outer circumstances and what is happening "out there", but what YOU are bringing with you in the form of your beliefs about yourself, about people, about the world, and about this magnificent universe we all inhabit.

Those beliefs will absolutely influence your experiences as a pilgrim in life, walking alone or with others, during or beyond your pilgrimage. They create the story you tell yourself about who you are and what you are capable of.

So, what do you believe about yourself?

Do you believe yourself incapable of making this kind of journey on your own; that you are too weak, too out-of-shape, too old (or too young), too filled with fear and doubt, too indecisive? That too many dangers await and can't be planned for, so it's better to be safe than sorry? Or do you believe that, step by step, you will make it? You have confidence in your ability to handle the unexpected and know that you will figure things out as you go along.

What do you believe about people?

Do you believe that they are essentially good, or bad? Can you trust strangers to help you out, or do you believe they will take advantage of you the moment you drop your guard or show any form of openness?

What do you believe about the world?

Is it a safe place or dangerous place? Do you walk in fear of the world, closed off, jealously guarding your possessions and looking upon all with suspicion? Or do you walk in curiosity of the world, seeking what connects you to others, rather than what divides you?

What do you believe about the world beyond the physical?

Are you all alone in this vast Universe, with no one to rely on or trust beyond yourself, or beyond what you can see and touch? Are you a small, insignificant being whose actions don't matter because you're only one person, and what can one person do? Or are you a powerful being, a magnificent creation, here to experience the world in all its grandeur and to unfold your greatest potential as a human being? And that, independent of your spiritual beliefs, or none, you are supported in your journey?

Again, there is no right or wrong answer here, but how you answer these questions will greatly determine your experiences during pilgrimage, especially when walking alone and you have no other safety net but your beliefs.

Ultimately, the biggest question you must answer is:

Am I walking in fear or in love?

Where will you choose to place your attention?

Prepare Today!

❖ Develop a new vocabulary of self-talk, with phrases such as:
  ◊ I believe in my ability to handle any situation.
  ◊ I believe that people are intrinsically good.
  ◊ I believe the world is a safe and friendly place.
  ◊ I believe I will receive what I need, when I need it.
  ◊ I believe in the gift of every difficulty, even when I can't see it right away.
  ◊ I bless the good in this situation.

Repeating these words to yourself is a powerful way of awakening a more expanded way of thinking.

You may find that repeating these words makes you feel hopeful, optimistic, happy, at peace. That is their purpose.

When you are able to re-frame how you see the world, the world will respond in kind. When you are at peace, you exude an energy which facilitates your journey, and brings to you all manner of unexpected experiences.

Many people expect those experiences to be exclusively positive. They may think that if they speak positive words, their experiences will always be positive. There are two things to be aware of:

1. The words are meant to evoke a FEELING. It is this feeling that begins to transform your thoughts into beliefs that are anchored in your body, in your very cells. It is the feeling that converts the concepts into a way of being.

2. When we declare that we believe <fill in the blank>, the entire Universe conspires to make you live that. Sometimes, that means experiencing the complete opposite, so that you may consciously CHOOSE this new belief and way of thinking. It's not a punishment

or a test, but an opportunity to put into practice the new beliefs you now proclaim.

If you are able to observe your reactions and interactions with enough emotional detachment, you will see what a wonderful game of self-discovery you are playing, where your very reality is based on what you believe.

Even if you respond only once in a new or expanded way, you are making tremendous progress. Congratulate yourself for not only challenging your beliefs but having the courage to live new ones.

❖   Make eye contact with a stranger
It may seem insignificant, but part of practicing your belief that people are good is to look AT people, not through them, past them or away from them. It requires us to crack the hardened shell we have erected to protect ourselves from what we believe to be a cruel world.

Start with something small, like the clerk at the grocery store. Smile, and say hello.

Standing in an elevator, say hello to just one person.

Or someone passing you by in your neighborhood, when you're out for a walk. If you can't greet them, at the very least, look them in the eye and nod in their general direction.

You will be walking with strangers from around the world on the Camino, or meeting people on pilgrimages beyond Spain. You may be walking alone. Standing in the confidence of what you believe and making eye contact are keys to dissolving barriers and making a human connection.

Ask yourself:

What do I believe about myself as an individual?

What do I believe about people?

What do I believe about the world?

What do I believe about the world beyond the physical?

Is there one thought or belief that stirs up feelings of anger, resentment, fear?

Am I open to the possibility of transforming that thought or belief into one that feels more positive for me, that brings me a sense of peace or release?

If so, what thought can I replace it with?

What am I prepared to do to hold on to this new way of thinking?

Develop a Resilient Mind

> Ideas and concepts are malleable and change all the time. They are only as fixed as we choose them to be.

As I mentioned earlier, your thoughts and beliefs create the story you tell yourself about who you are and what you are capable of doing. Creating a new story based on different beliefs is a journey all its own, and it begins with being open to the possibility that there is another way of seeing yourself and your world; that it is possible to change how you think and what you believe.

The mind performs a crucial role: to create a sense of security and predictability in our lives. You feel safe because you know what to expect. There are no surprises. Information about the world comes in through your senses; your mind interprets it based on past experiences, and files it away under similar experiences. That's why there's comfort in our routine. Your mind is a wonderful storehouse of past experiences.

But what happens when we are in completely new and undefined situations? The mind scrambles to fit it into a category it recognizes and when it can't, we begin to feel anxious and afraid. We close off, wanting to retreat into the safety of what we know, because we can't interpret this new data based on our old beliefs and ideas.

Also, because there is so much information for the mind to capture, it can't do it all. So, how does it choose? Based on what it already knows and its habitual way of thinking. At any one time, there are a myriad of simultaneous events occurring, but you can only capture what you focus on; and often, we focus on what already know.

In the now infamous Selective Attention Test performed by Daniel Simons and Christopher Chabris, viewers were instructed to watch a video where two teams, one in white shirts and the other in black shirts, pass a basketball back and forth. When asked to count the number of passes made by the white-shirt team only, their results were usually accurate; but more than half of the viewers failed to see one important element: the woman in the gorilla suit who walks amongst the teams, thumps her chest, remains in view for ten seconds, and then walks off camera.

That's right, more than half of the viewers did not see the gorilla and argued vociferously against it, until they were shown the clip again.

To watch this video, and read about similar stories, visit their website http://theinvisiblegorilla.com.

You will see what you focus on. The journey, therefore, becomes about training the mind to identify new, unknown experiences, and recognize them as opportunities for growth and expansion in thinking. New neural pathways are created in your physical brain when you are able to embrace the gifts of the unknown rather than be paralyzed by them.

If you are able to do this, you develop a resilient mind, one that is capable of responding with ease.

You become more confident in your ability to handle an unknown.

You tap into knowledge and wisdom that you didn't know you had.

Your pilgrimage becomes the means to expand, not limit, your perspectives.

How can you begin to retrain your mind?

There are so many schools of thought when it comes to the mind and its workings, and many books written on the subject. At the end of this section, I list a few resources.

On one end are teachings that advocate using techniques to stop the mind from thinking, to come to a place of stillness where any thoughts that arise are allowed to simply float by without analysis or attachment. You merely observe them and let them pass. The eventual goal is to become completely detached from your thoughts, and therefore, free from suffering.

On the other end are teachings that advocate using affirmations, phrases that you repeat to yourself over and again, essentially re-wiring your brain by creating new neural pathways, and retraining it to think new thoughts that bring a sense of peace, calm and well-being…thus opening doorways to new experiences.

I have practiced both techniques, and many in between, and encourage you to explore this fascinating terrain of the mind.

Whichever technique you choose, I encourage you to adopt an attitude of childlike discovery and play, as it's all too easy to become frustrated when we don't see immediate results and to not only dismiss the teachings, but to judge ourselves as being incapable of change. It takes great courage to challenge your beliefs in the first place, so applaud yourself for taking up this challenge.

The bridge between these worlds is love.

I have learned to speak to myself in very loving terms when I am trying to transform an aspect of my thinking that brings up feelings of guilt, torment, fear, anger, etc. into ones that make me feel at peace, confident, alive, trusting, energized.

I speak to my mind as if I am speaking to a child whom I deeply love, with the understanding that change is a process, and that with great patience, compassion and perseverance, all is possible.

I see my mind as one very important element of a self that is whole, balanced, healthy and integrated. It's not something to dominate, set aside or transcend. It is a powerful instrument to use in the service of a self and a heart that is growing into its full potential.

As such, I practice loving kindness with my own process of transformation.

I congratulate myself when I choose a new thought in a situation.

I celebrate my victories, large and small.

I thank my mind for making this transition with me, and being such a loving instrument of my highest ideals and plans that I have for my life.

I have seen how this approach brings about the change in thinking a lot more quickly and powerfully than judging myself.

It creates a mind that is resilient, flexible and continually expanding.

It makes for a life-long learner.

Prepare Today!

Browse the aisles of the Self-help and Personal Growth section of any library or bookstore, perhaps even online, and you will find a plethora of books and videos to choose from. Although these are some of my recommendations, allow yourself to be drawn to the books that most connect with you. I speak about following intuition in the next section, but allow that feeling to guide you.

Authors who have influenced my way of thinking:
- ◊   Neale Donald Walsch
- ◊   Eckhart Tolle
- ◊   Deepak Chopra
- ◊   Dr. Wayne Dyer
- ◊   Louise L. Hay
- ◊   Abraham-Hicks
- ◊   Jose Silva
- ◊   Paramahansa Yogananda
- ◊   Susan Jeffers
- ◊   Shakti Gawain

Movies to explore:

◊ What the bleep do we know?
◊ The Secret
◊ The Matrix
◊ Way of the Peaceful Warrior
◊ You can Heal your Life
◊ Water Crystals in Motion: Messages from Water
◊ The Connected Universe (Nassim Haramein)

Manage your Expectations

We are often our own worst critics, condemning ourselves when our experiences don't measure up to our expectations of them.

Whether they are conscious or unconscious, we all have expectations around what our pilgrimage should look like, how our plans should unfold, what it means to be an "authentic" pilgrim, or how people should behave.

Often, these expectations are based on the experiences and stories of other pilgrims, and can set us up for disappointment when our personal journey does not look like their text-book experience.

> Our expectations close us up and prevent us from seeing the world of possibilities before us.

It's easy to say "release your expectations", but infinitely more challenging to put into practice.

If your journey is not unfolding as you had planned, and you feel frustrated or disappointed, one thing that may help you feel better right away is to stop the complaining and judging. That alone is a huge step in making peace with your expectations.

I would also invite you to consider that this is perhaps EXACTLY how YOUR pilgrimage needs to unfold because this is what YOU need to experience at this moment, to grow personally, mentally, emotionally and spiritually.

If you can, begin to reflect on the gifts that your pilgrimage has provided you so far.

Give thanks for what you have learned and, although it may not look like anyone else's, it is absolutely perfect for you and is serving your highest good.

I had very rigid ideas of what it meant to be an authentic pilgrim. To me, that meant walking everywhere. No buses. No taxis. No rides of any kind. It meant carrying my backpack at all times. In my mind, only walking made a true pilgrim.

During my walk to Jerusalem, where I expected to walk in that authentic way, there were occasions when people drove us to their homes for meals or to spend the night, and I always justified those by saying that it was out of our way and so were acceptable.

After almost ten months of walking, we were finally in Turkey. We entered on a three-month visitor visa, fully expecting to clear the country in that time. We didn't count on the longer distances between towns, the many nooks and crannies that make up the Turkish coastline, and the blistering summer heat that sapped our energies, all of which delayed our journey.

Our three-month visas expired, and the only way to renew them was to take a ferry from Alanya to neighboring Cyprus, spend a night, then re-enter Turkey and ask for a new visa.

I was prepared to take the ferry at Alanya, but then we were given the option to return either to Alanya, or another coastal town called Tasucu, about 250 kilometers (155 miles) further ahead. In between, the towns were more widely dispersed, making for 50-km (31-mile) day walks, with little to no possibility for water or shelter from the heat.

The "authentic pilgrim" in me demanded that we take the ferry back to Alanya, and walk to Tasucu. I had already walked 4,000 kilometers (almost 2,500 miles) by then, yet still felt the need to reach for a level of perfection that only existed in my mind.

I decided it was time to make peace with that inner perfectionist – that inner dictator – who was demanding I fulfill some arbitrary and completely unrealistic definition of what it means to be a pilgrim.

My heart knew that I was a pilgrim. I needed to bring my mind along to embrace this more expanded concept of a pilgrim being defined not by the number of kilometers or miles that they walk, but by the intention that they carry in their heart and what they contribute to the path they walk.

My feelings of guilt at returning to Tasucu were not assuaged right away, and I had to practice a great deal of self-love and positive self-talk; but after a few days of walking, I found a freedom and a lightness that had, until then, eluded me.

I repeated positive, affirming phrases to myself such as:

◊ Look at everything that you have learned about yourself.
◊ Look at all the emotional pain you have looked at and made peace with.
◊ Look at how far you have come in your personal journey of understanding.
◊ Look at how many kilometers you've already walked!
◊ Look at how your body and your feet are still carrying you forward after almost a year of walking.
◊ Look at the courage you've already shown in so many situations.
◊ Look at all the times you have led with wisdom.
◊ Look at all the seeds of love that you have planted with others along the way, and look at all the love you have already received.

Looking at how far I've already journeyed – physically, mentally, emotionally and spiritually – and focusing my energies on the gained, as opposed to the missed, were the keys to helping me over the hurdle of expectations.

Ask yourself:

What expectations do I have from my pilgrimage?

What is their source? My own inner dictates and desire for growth, or the experiences of others I have read about?

Do these ideas bring a sense of enthusiasm or foreboding?

Do they make me feel light or heavy? Do they sound extreme or just right for me?

Do I believe that this is what I "should" do, or is this what my heart is calling me to do?

What words can I state to myself to make peace with my inner perfectionist?

Practice Acceptance

Walking in any country foreign to our own is going to bring us face to face with values and ideas that may be quite contrary to ours. We may not like those ideas or agree with them, but we must respect and accept them.

This is especially difficult when walking in countries where religious or cultural traditions and freedoms collide with our own.

When I walked in Muslim countries, or places where Islam was the dominant religion, I followed their norms. I wore long-sleeved shirts and a floor-length skirt.

When I entered a mosque, I covered my head. When I didn't know what to do, I asked and found that by showing interest in, and respect for, their traditions, rather than judgment and fear, I was similarly met with interest and respect.

It was altogether tempting to impose my ideas on them, but I found greater connection with others when I was able to listen deeply and ask with respect. The conversations that developed opened my mind to perspectives I had never considered. That still doesn't mean that I agreed with them, but I most certainly did walk away with a deeper understanding and appreciation of the situation. I also made a human connection that went beyond stereotypes and generalizations, and that established a foundation for an open, respectful exchange of ideas.

This is a daily, moment by moment, practice.

There will always be situations and perspectives that we disagree with. How we respond, however, is completely in our hands.

No one can tell me how to think or what to feel. I am in absolute control of my thoughts and feelings; and that is perhaps the greatest power we possess: the power to choose what to think, what to feel and how to respond.

When our pilgrimage took us into southern Lebanon, land of Hezbollah and Muslim extremism, I became quite afraid. The further south we walked, the more unsafe I felt. At one of our stops, we found ourselves alone in a large coffee shop with two very intense-looking Arab men who kept staring at us and the sign on our backpack which said "Walking for Peace" in Arabic.

Eventually, one of them spat out bitterly, "Go tell the Americans about peace, not us."

Everything inside of me froze. Here I was, a Lebanese woman technically in my own homeland where I spoke the language and understood the culture, yet terrified at where this conversation could lead.

Alberto was decidedly more self-assured than I at the moment, and with calm authority responded, "You are judging us before even knowing us. We would be happy to sit with you and share our story."

The men stared hard at us for a while, but eventually invited us to their table. We explained the nature of our pilgrimage, where we had walked, how we had walked and much more. We clarified that we had carried our message of peace through eleven countries, and that it wasn't intended solely for them. We didn't speak about politics, but about creating inner peace in order to work more effectively for outer peace.

In that, they quickly agreed, adding that the Koran values this seeking of inner peace.

Although they wanted to speak about the political injustices and atrocities, we didn't go there with them. We listened with respect and compassion, and not once judged who was right or wrong. We tried to impress upon them what our experiences had taught us: that you empower what you fight against, and that the key to building peace is to make peace with the inner tyrant first and work from there to build the world you wish to live in.

It was a very candid discussion, an exchange that I

never would have imagined possible with men who held such extremist views. I wasn't sure that we had changed their ideas about conspiracy theories and the need for radical action, but I was certain that we had touched them personally. Somewhere in that exchange, I knew that the message of peace would work its way into their lives.

When we mentioned our excitement at crossing this final border from Lebanon into Israel and reaching Jerusalem, they asked us to pray for them there, a request that touched us deeply and that we honored upon our arrival.

This is one of the great gifts of pilgrimage: the opportunity to put into practice ideas that transform and inspire us, and in consequence, those around us.

Practice Today!

Meet with someone whose ideas, culture or religion differs from your own. Approach them with curiosity and respect. Ask them to tell you their story, why they believe what they believe. Truly listen to them, not only with your ears but with your whole body. Don't interrupt. Ask questions. Breathe deeply through it all, especially those parts you disagree with. Allow them to speak fully, and to complete their sentences. Receive this information not solely into your mind, but into your heart. Thank them for allowing you to understand. Congratulate yourself for having the courage to step out of your comfort zone and build bridges with those whose ideas differ from your own.

Mony Dojeiji

PREPARING THE EMOTIONAL JOURNEY

5 PREPARING THE EMOTIONAL JOURNEY

Physical and mental preparations will calm the mind, but to walk alone, you must learn to calm your fears, especially the fear of the unknown. It is the fears that heighten anxiety and throw our emotions, along with our balance and perspective, into frenzy.

At the same time, whether consciously or unconsciously, other people begin to project their fears and judgments upon us. Without meaning to, we take on their fears and make them our own, believing that their experiences will translate into ours.

It is an active effort, and tremendous act of self-love, to remain centered in YOUR beliefs of "other people", and to only allow YOUR experiences to determine YOUR beliefs.

When you learn to control your emotions, you begin to hear the whispers of that small still voice within you, the place where your truth resides and that is waiting to guide you on your journey.

How do you calm your fears and emotions?

Breathe!
It may seem obvious, but breathe.

Slowly. Deliberately. Consciously.

Into the very core of your belly.

Inhale deeply. Exhale fully.

Place one hand on your belly and one hand on your heart.

Breathe into your hands and allow the breath to steady your emotions.

The longer you practice this type of breathing, the more naturally you will breathe in this way all the time.

Breathing in this way has the added benefit of focusing your attention on the present moment and giving the mind a rest, all of which calm the emotions and bring you to a place of clarity, from which new ideas and possibilities can emerge.

Acknowledge the Fear

Acknowledge that this fear exists. Acknowledge the emotions. Resisting, ignoring or burying them will only keep them there.

What you resist, persists!

So, better to acknowledge the presence of this energy within you than allow it to dominate or take over.

In the same way that I speak with my mind, I also speak with my fears. I understand them to be parts of me that are showing me a deep pain or distress that has occurred in my life and which now require my attention and my love in order to heal.

I believe that the situations that cause these fears to emerge are my deepest self's way of letting me know that there is something within me that is ready to be looked at. While it's inside me, I can't identify it. But the situation I'm facing that has made me feel afraid is the perfect way to see it.

Obviously if you're in a situation where you feel your life may be in danger, you get away!

But the true inner work of healing the fear and pain is to acknowledge its presence within you, and with great self-love and self-compassion, begin the process of transforming it.

Transform the Fear

One of my favorite techniques for transforming fear is called Ho'oponopono, an ancient teaching used by Hawaiian shamans or healers. I have used it consistently for the past decade and have seen tremendous results.

The premise of the teaching is that I am 100% responsible for what is in my life; that what appears in my experience is there because I have put it there, consciously or unconsciously; that thoughts aren't so much the problem as the underlying emotions, memories and energies that we attach to them; and that these energies (such as fear) vibrate within me and attract a like energy through Law of Attraction i.e. like attracts like. To learn more about this universal law, I invite you to investigate the teachings of Abraham-Hicks.

> So, to heal the outside,
> we must first heal the inside.

I had a hard time with this teaching in the beginning because I saw no end. Does that mean I'm responsible for the earthquakes around the world? For the revolutions? The famines? The droughts? Where does it end?

The teaching would say yes, but I'm not ready to go that far yet. I will tell you that I have applied this teaching to resolve personal fears and conflicts with others, and have seen that it works. The grand majority of my fears can be summed up as the fear of what other people think of me.

In working with this teaching for many years now, I have added my personal lens to make it fit my philosophy of life. I have come to understand that the difficult experiences of my life that repeat themselves are not there to torture me, but to give me yet another opportunity to heal them. They are my own soul's crying out for liberation from its self-inflicted pain. They come from the highest place of love to serve me in my journey of liberation from fears or limits of any kind.

But the work of healing is mine alone. No one can free me but myself.

And self-love is the greatest liberator.

That is why the first words in Ho'oponopono are:

I love you.
I say those words to myself. I am giving this love to me. The obsessive, fear-filled self-talk can go on endlessly, but the moment I say "I love you, exactly as you are with all your fears and perceived failings," I open a space for a new energy to circulate within me.

I repeat the words "I love you" over and again, until I begin to feel a calm wash over me.

"I'm not sure where this fear comes from, whether it originated in this lifetime or another; but that doesn't matter. It's here. It's a part of me that I see, that I accept, that I love.

Mony, I love you as you are.

I'm sorry for whatever has caused this fear. I am sorry for any erroneous or mistaken belief, thought, feeling or emotion within me that has manifested in this difficult experience I'm now dealing with.

Please forgive me.
I didn't know how else to respond. I didn't know how else to feel or to think. I didn't know any better. I did the best that I knew how at that moment. But it's all right. I'm learning. I'm growing. I'm bound to make mistakes. When I know better, I'll do better.

Mony, I love you."

This self-forgiveness is a key tenet of the teaching. Again, I'm speaking to myself. I'm not asking God or any power outside of me for forgiveness because, in my belief system, God is Love and does not need that I ask for forgiveness. I am loved as I am, period.

In the beginning, I found it difficult and uncomfortable to speak to myself in this way. It didn't feel good or natural to give myself so much love and forgiveness. How telling!

With time and practice, however, I began to feel compassion for myself and to see myself as a child who needs understanding, patience and a great deal of love as they journey in their life. I began to soften my stance towards myself, to be less demanding and harsh in my judgments of myself.

Thank you.

This is the final element of the teaching.

"Thank you, fear, for revealing yourself to me.

Thank you, person or situation, for taking on that role so that I may see my fear.

Thank you to my own Higher Self - the wisest, most eternal part of me – for showing me this fear.

Thank you me (Mony) for demonstrating the willingness and courage to explore and transform your deepest fears; and to continue advancing on this amazing and sometimes scary adventure in the unknown that is life. You deserve my highest admiration and respect, Mony. I love you! Thank you!

Thank you, Universe, for the opportunity to heal this, to free myself of this weight in my heart, my body, my emotions, my thoughts.

Thank you for the opportunity to allow more Light to enter and fill this void.

Thank you for the opportunity to soar.

I now ask Love to transform this energy of fear (this limited, erroneous belief about life), to return it to its natural state, which is Light. This Light now permeates every cell of my body, permeates my thoughts, my emotions. I vibrate with this Light. I am this Light.

I now cut all ties with those who may have contributed to this fear from the beginning of creation to the end of all time and, with great love and thanks, allow them to continue their journey. I am free.

Thank you, thank you, thank you.

My inner world is safe and in harmony.

In my inner world, all is healed, whole and holy.

I walk the world with confidence and openness

From my heart, I project this inner harmony and peace to the world."

By loving myself, by feeling worthy of that Love, by apologizing to myself for any undesired thought, feeling or action, by forgiving myself for it, and then thanking myself for the opportunity to heal and integrate what has kept me small and fear-filled, I am finally free to walk the world fear-less.

If remnants of the fear creep back in, then I repeat the key elements, not necessarily word for word or in the same order, but always striving for the feeling of liberation and certainty that I felt the first time.

It's a technique that has consistently worked for me, and that I encourage you to try.

There is no formal website for this teaching, but you can Google Dr. Len Hew, the modern founder of this teaching, along with SITH (Self Identity through Ho'oponopono).

Emotional Sustenance

Emotional support is different from emotional sustenance. It is healthy and vital to turn to others to support us in our journeys when we feel we cannot continue alone; but asking others to fill us with what we lack is dependence.

The continual need for validation often masks feelings of insecurity, self-doubt and low self-worth. When we look to others to provide us with the love, respect and confidence we lack, we may risk alienating those providing it and miss an opportunity to nurture these aspects within ourselves.

You will be making choices and decisions – including walking alone – that not everyone will support or agree with. Learning to look inwards for your emotional sustenance takes courage and a great deal of self-love.

This is a lifetime journey for many. Of course, there are many techniques which I invite you to investigate. One of the simplest and most powerful practices I know is a derivative of Ho'oponopono. All you need to do is say the words "I love you" to yourself, as often as you can.

◊ To the lonely one grasping at love, no matter how hurtful it feels: I love you.
◊ To the frightened one choosing safety over pursuing a dream: I love you.
◊ To the rejected one feeling he/she will never be good enough: I love you.
◊ To the one angry at life: I love you.
◊ To the one frustrated by indecision: I love you.
◊ To the hurt and betrayed one: I love you.
◊ To the inner tormentor who mocks my efforts: I love you.

Walking alone demands that you be light emotionally. This practice puts you directly on the path of facing those emotional blockages that keep you small and transforming them into a power and confidence you can now use on your journey.

Those three simple words release you, and lift the burdens you have been carrying. They are a powerful elixir that have the power to knit those splintered parts of ourselves into one healthy, healed whole, using love.

You are embarking on a grand journey, out of your comfort zone, and into so many unknowns. Give yourself credit for having the audacity to dream that big, and to take steps towards achieving that dream. Of course you will go through trials on your journey, and that's a good thing. You want these challenges, so that you are stretched to reflect on who you are as a person, what you choose to believe and how you will act in consequence. There will be moments when despair and frustration will take hold, and you will want to give up or, worse, judge yourself as being incapable of making it. The words "I love you" bring you back onto the path and give you the courage you need to take one more step.

If you can, I invite you to look in the mirror and repeat those three words to yourself. Many would rather do anything but that!

Yet, it is the key to liberating all that keeps us small, and to giving us wings and courage to fly alone.

Walking alone means loving ourselves as we are, and remembering that we are pilgrims on the journey of life.

I share with you now a passage that I long ago committed to memory and that I repeat to myself every now and again when I find my courage flagging.

Our deepest fear is not that we are inadequate. Our deepest fear is that we are powerful beyond measure.

It is our light, not our darkness that most frightens us.

We ask ourselves, Who am I to be brilliant, gorgeous, talented, fabulous?

Actually, who are you not to be?

You are a child of God.

Your playing small does not serve the world.

There is nothing enlightened about shrinking so that other people won't feel insecure around you.

We are all meant to shine, as children do.

We were born to make manifest the glory of God that is within us. It's not just in some of us; it's in everyone.

And as we let our own light shine, we unconsciously give other people permission to do the same.

As we are liberated from our own fear, our presence automatically liberates others.

(From, A Return to Love: Reflections on the Principles of "A Course in Miracles", Ch. 7, Section 3 (1992), p. 190 by Marianne Williamson)

Develop your Inner Senses

We are raised and trained to believe that we can only trust our outer senses. If we can't see it, hear it, smell it, taste it or touch it in the outside world, it does not exist.

But if you examine words such as IN-spiration, IN-sight, IN-tuition, you will see that they all begin with the word "in", meaning there is something that exists INSIDE of us that we are completely ignoring.

Intuition means to know something without any proof or evidence; a feeling that guides a person to act a certain way without fully understanding why.

Insight literally means "inner sight", the ability to see into a situation and intuitively understand its nature.

Inspiration means a sudden brilliant, creative, or timely idea.

When you're "in touch" with something or someone, you have an intuitive or empathetic awareness.

When you "tune in", you're listening to not only what's being said, but capturing nuances that go beyond what is physically heard.

In the same way that pilgrims trust the yellow arrows of the Camino to lead them to their destination, developing your inner senses allows you to begin trusting your inner yellow arrows – your own inner guidance system – to show you the way, on and off the pilgrimage path. It is the key to walking alone with confidence, especially when there are no outer yellow arrows to show you the way.

We ALL have this deep wisdom within us. If you can learn to tap into it, it will let you know, in each moment of your life, what you need to be aware of and what you need to do.

This wisdom is accessed through intuition.

Sadly, we don't trust our intuition, and immediately dismiss "a hunch" or a "gut feeling". We have been taught to look externally for our answers, and to trust the outer authority, someone smarter, wiser and certainly braver than us.

Of course it's good to get help, guidance and support from other people – and there are people who may have knowledge and information that we need – but, when it comes right down to it, only you know what's right for you. Only you know the path that you alone must walk.

By all means, listen to what the "experts" have to say, including what you're reading right now, but then check in with yourself and ask:

> Does this feel true and right for me?

I'm not saying disregard logic, but BALANCE it by checking in and asking yourself if the decision you are making feels true and right for you.

As I mentioned earlier, the mind is like a big computer which has stored information based on previous experiences, collected from your physical senses. It's great if you don't have to face new situations, but because pilgrimage gets you outside of all that you know, then you need something else to check with.

Intuition taps into all the wisdom, knowledge and information within you, and in the universe, and brings you just the piece that you need at this moment.

So, how do you develop your intuition?

Steps to Developing Intuition

Countless books have been written on developing your intuition and senses beyond the physical five. Essentially, the steps are:
- Quiet the mind
- Focus inwards
- Ask your question
- Pay attention
- Act
- Give thanks

Quiet the Mind

To listen to your intuition, and develop your other senses, you must learn to quiet your mind and move your attention to your body. It requires you to be still, completely immersed in the present moment, fully taking in what is happening in your surroundings.

You must S-L-O-W down and begin to BREATHE deeply.

Breathing is possibly the most effective tool for slowing down your mind and bringing your attention to your body. If you can master deep, full breathing, especially during moments when you need clarity and direction, you will have taken a giant leap in connecting with your intuition.

You can also go for a short walk, do some light yoga, listen to relaxing music, take a hot bath, meditate... whatever works for you to get you into a relaxed, receptive state, where your mind is slowed down and you are in touch with your body.

Even during pilgrimage, surrounded by people, you can still find a quiet spot to practice what I am suggesting.

Focus Inwards

Shift your attention from your mind to your body, especially the heart. Use your mind's eye, visualize the energy that is in your mind now moving down to your heart and your gut/abdomen. Feel the relaxation invading your body, and your mind at stillness. Feel ready to receive.

Ask your Question

Once in that state, ask yourself questions such as:

◊ What do I need to know at this moment?
◊ Which way should I go?
◊ How do I resolve this situation?

The first question is a great one because it's general, and gently opens the door for your intuition to send you any kind of message, thought, feeling or awareness that you need to have in the moment.

If you have a specific question, or an issue you wish to get some clarity on, simply ask to be shown what you need.

Develop your own way of connecting with your intuition. Some people like to light a candle or burn some incense. Others prefer the solitude and quiet of a dark room. Still others can only connect when walking in nature. You must find the way that works for you.

It may seem artificial at first. You may not believe that anything will happen. You may not even trust the process. But I can assure you that the more you practice connecting with your own wisdom, the more you will develop the process that works for you.

Pay Attention to what comes up.

You may get a feeling, an image or a sudden flash of understanding and clarity.

Something may catch your attention that you hadn't noticed before.

You overhear a conversation that seems connected to what you're dealing with.

You see the same word over and again.

A butterfly flies in a certain direction.

The light hits the path in a unique way.

A pilgrim walks up to you and joins you and you strike up a conversation.

You turn on the radio or listen to a podcast and hear something related to your question.

You open a book or read an article that is connected to the issue.

There are an infinite number of ways in which the clarity or answer may come to you.

Sometimes, the impressions, feelings or thoughts may not make sense to you, but that's okay. Stay with them. Don't try to figure them out right away. Don't judge or dismiss whatever arises. Write them down if you can. Stay open. Let the answer come to you.

At other times, you may not get anything at all, or at least not anything that seems particularly relevant or powerful. That okay too. Don't try to force it. If you feel yourself getting frustrated, then stop and go do something else. What you need to know will usually come to you later, and quite often, when you're not looking for it.

In the middle of preparing your meal, you may get a flash of insight.

As you're walking by yourself or speaking with someone, you see something or speak with someone that gives you the answer you need.

You may walk past a café and something irresistible pulls you to go inside, even when logic dictates you should continue on your way and not waste any time. You'll walk inside, where you'll be drawn to a particular object or poster or conversation, and right there, you will receive exactly what you need.

That's how our intuition works. It's always with you, guiding you, nudging you in the direction of your highest good and the next thing that you need to learn.

You know it's your intuition because you feel alive.

There's an energy that courses through you. Your heart may begin to race. There's a knowing and a certainty. There's also calm. As you develop your relationship with your intuition, you will also begin to understand the cues it is using to confirm its presence.

<u>Act</u> on the messages from your intuition, even when the mind protests that it makes no logical sense. Do it anyways.

Start small.

Don't do something drastic because you think maybe your intuition is telling you to do so.

Start with the seemingly insignificant decisions such as: What should I have for dinner? Should I call my friend? Where should I go out tonight?

Take a moment. Breathe. Check in. Ask yourself: does this feel right for me?

<u>Give Thanks</u> for what you have received.

Thank your intuition for giving you the answers you seek.

Thank your intuition for the deepening connection that you have, and commit to strengthening it.

Remember...

Fear makes you want to control every detail. You feel anxious and stressed when you can't work out every detail beforehand, and become exponentially so when your plans go awry.

But...

When you can be in stillness, looking inwards for your answers and attentive to what arises within, you begin to feel empowered, confident in where you are right now.

You begin to trust your own inner yellow arrows.

You can see the next step more clearly, and so step into it with greater confidence.

You develop resilience, and are able to flow with the unexpected with grace and ease rather than be defeated by it.

It is then that the miracles and magic begin to happen.

To me, this connection with intuition is the most important relationship that I have in my life, one that I practiced unfailingly during my pilgrimages, and that I continue to develop to this day.

My book is filled with examples of following my intuition, but I will share one that happened very recently, far from pilgrimage.

I had been thinking about learning how to produce videos so that I could tell video stories, and lamenting not being able to find any online courses that I liked. In the tasks of my day-to-day, I eventually forgot all about it.

During this time, I began practicing yoga daily, watching a program on my local television station, Rogers TV. During every break came the announcement to volunteer at Rogers to learn all about show production. In a flash, it hit me! I felt it in my gut. I could volunteer and get the hands-on experience I needed. I knew this was the way, but I had so many projects on the go and work to do that I dismissed it as well.

But the feeling that I should pursue this persisted.

Finally, I submitted my application. I was called for an interview and immediately began working in the production room. I learned a great deal and, within a few months of being there, auditioned for the position of on-air host and producer of one of the shows. I was terrified, but everything within me was pushing me to overcome my fears and do it anyways. Even though I had no formal training as a host, I discovered that I did possess an ability that I never appreciated: storytelling and interviewing.

My experience on the show would open many more doors in the media storytelling world, and land me as host of my own show called "The Author's Journey". They would also give me the confidence to eventually record my own series of video stories called "The Pilgrim Story Hour" on Facebook.

The message is obvious: listen to those insistent feelings that are pulling you down a path that you may rationally consider a waste of time.

It is your intuition nudging you in the direction of your growth and highest good.

Allow Others to Walk their Own Path

Walking alone sometimes means having the courage to leave behind those who simply don't understand us or support our dreams.

It is curious that our pilgrimages often bring other peoples' fears and opinions to the forefront, and we are at times left unprepared for their less-than-enthusiastic response. As much as we long for those we love to join us in our excitement, there are times they simply cannot, and we are left having to decide what to do.

> The most difficult part of any personal journey is honoring your path and following your calling while, with great love and compassion, allowing others to follow theirs.

In my case, with all their best intentions, some friends and family did not support my decision to quit my job, and certainly not my decision to walk the Camino or to Jerusalem. They simply could not understand my choices and, as much as they loved me, only wanted me back inside the box that they were comfortable having me in. It was at times difficult speaking with them because it felt as if we were on two different planets.

I had to learn to stop looking for their approval and validation, and to trust my path and my decisions, even when they didn't make sense to anyone else or meet with their approval.

It was difficult in the beginning but, with time, new people began entering my life. I could be my authentic self, and they embraced that.

I have no doubt the same will happen with you.

In situations like this, Ho'oponopono can be a great tool to release those individuals – and yourself – from these sometimes unhealthy bonds.

Surround yourself with positive and supportive people

today, for they will help you before, during and after your pilgrimage.

Ask yourself:

Who is excited about my pilgrimage, and supports me?

Who is holding me back, trying to dissuade me from following my dream, making sarcastic or double-edged comments, and placing fear in my heart?

Am I prepared to allow them to live their story of fear and limitation alone? If yes, what steps can I take to separate myself from them?

If not, what's holding me back? Ho'oponopono is a powerful technique to heal whatever comes up here. Then, explore what you can do to separate yourself from them, with love.

Am I prepared to explore my story of possibilities? If not, what's holding me back? Again, Ho'oponopono is a powerful technique here. Then, explore what you can do to separate yourself from them, with love.

What steps will I take now to dwell in that space of possibility, always?

PREPARING THE SPIRITUAL
JOURNEY

6 PREPARING THE SPIRITUAL JOURNEY

Matters of the spirit are perhaps the most difficult for pilgrims to speak about.

We all have our unique reasons for being on pilgrimage. There is something that calls us to embark on this quest, even when we can't articulate it in words. It is a drive that is beyond simply going for a walk because, if we really only wanted to go for a walk, most of our countries have wonderful parks, beaches and hiking trails that we can easily choose rather than traveling (often overseas) to walk a pilgrimage path to a sacred destination.

So, what is it that pulls us to be pilgrims, and not merely hikers or walkers?

To me, there is a part of us here on earth that longs for a connection that goes beyond the material. We long to touch the stars, be that drop in the ocean, connect with our ancestors, form a part of the beauty and grace that surrounds us. We want to feel a magic and wonder that transcends our physical senses. It comes as a silent, insistent whisper or as a clamoring, ferocious roar. That insistent calling will not be silenced or denied, and will eventually open our hearts and call us to pilgrimage.

And that calling transcends and includes all religions, faiths and beliefs.

Pilgrimage is a sacred journey, made to a sacred location, but the most sacred of destinations is to that part of you that longs for transcendence, for connection, for meaning.

That, to me, is the spiritual quest and what pilgrimage offers you, if you are open to the possibility.

Questions about the nature of our existence have been asked since time immemorial:

◊ Who am I?
◊ Why am I here?
◊ What is my purpose?
◊ Does God exist? What is God?
◊ Is everything random, or is there some meaning to events in the world?

These and many more questions have driven seekers from all faiths and traditions to find the answers that will fill the void that rational thought alone often cannot do.

And only you can answer those questions.

People can guide you, show you a way, but only by going inwards can you begin to formulate the answers that will guide your life's journey, on and off a pilgrimage path.

My Spiritual Beliefs

I have come to these beliefs over time, after putting them to the test in the laboratory of my pilgrimages and life experiences. They form the essence of who I am as a person, and inform how I move about in this world.

I believe we are eternal beings on a journey of continual exploration, who have chosen this physical body to play.

I believe our true nature is indescribably beautiful, radiant, pure, perfect, loving, wise and powerful. You can call it Spirit, Highest Self, Divine Essence, Creator, Eternal Self, God, Light, or any other name that resonates with you.

I believe we are here to fully embody those highest aspects of ourselves, and to bring them into the world using our unique gifts, in the service of the good of all.

I respect all paths and religions, and when pressed, will say that my religion is Love because my experiences have demonstrated to me that Love is the essence of all existence. It is the essence of who I believe each and every one of us is.

Including you.

Those beliefs drive my decisions and choices. I see the world through that lens of unity, connection, oneness. At a fundamental level, I believe that what I say or do to the "other", I am saying and doing to myself, and so I am vigilant and conscious of my actions and the words I put forth.

What Story do you Believe?

I asked this question earlier: what do you believe about who you are?

You can, of course, choose to believe the story of separation; that you are alone in this vast Universe; that you can't trust anyone besides yourself; that you have to look out for number one and take all that you can get; that nothing exists beyond what you can see and touch.

And that will, of course, be your experience.

You can also choose to believe another story.

That you are deeply loved, simply because you exist on this Earth.

That there is nothing you have to do or be in order to earn or have this Love.

That even your most heinous thoughts, words and acts are absorbed and absolved in this great theatre you play in while here on Earth.

That, even if you don't remember or agree, your true nature is divine, ever-wise, ever-expanding into grander, more love-filled versions of itself.

That what drives this expansion is Love: universal, all-encompassing, ever-present.

It doesn't need that you know it, acknowledge it or even believe in it.

But it sure does make your life easier if you do.

All it wishes is to make itself known to you.

It won't impose itself on you. It won't ask for sacrifices of any kind. It awaits patiently, its hand always extended.

However, you will only see it when you begin to believe that it exists.

> *Credendo Vides*
> It is by believing that one sees.

It is up to you to initiate this relationship.

In the same way that you develop a relationship with your intuition and non-physical senses, so too can you begin to develop a relationship with that infinite part of yourself.

What would happen if you chose to believe this story of who you are?

Synchronicity – Language of the Universe

The Universe speaks to us through coincidences, synchronicities, repetitive patterns, numerical sequences, dreams, and all the soft, untouchable aspects that we simply have not been trained to notice. If anything, we are trained to dismiss them, just like our intuition.

This is a Universal Language of archetypes and symbols that is filled with meaning, and that is highly personalized. A dog can be a universal symbol of loyalty and friendship to me, but of danger and fear to you.

You must develop your personal lexicon and assign the meaning these symbols have for you.

You will intuitively know whether or not it's true. Your body will feel alive, electric, at peace, calm, confident, knowing. If you have been working on listening to your intuition, you will understand your body's cues and can use intuition to validate the message.

The harder work will be for you to suspend your judgments and disbelief, and to trust.

◊ Trust that this is the Universe's (or your Higher Self's) way of communicating with you.
◊ Trust that this is not merely your overactive imagination.
◊ Trust that you will interpret it correctly.
◊ Trust what your intuition is telling you about this so-called random event.
◊ Trust where the path is leading you.
◊ Trust where the highest Love is leading you.
◊ Trust yourself.

Practice Today!

Write down your dreams.

Keep a journal by your bed and, as soon as you wake up, try to remember the dream, noting as many details as possible. Don't look at it literally, but rather as a series of symbols trying to tell you a story. What does each element (person, animal, situation, environment, etc.) mean to you? What does it represent? What does it remind you of? What feeling does it evoke? Locked inside these symbols are the messages that your subconscious – or higher self – is trying to convey to you, helping you gain clarity and direction in your life.

Even nightmares serve this same divine purpose, showing you the beliefs, ideas or traumas that need your attention, your love. They offer invaluable clues to the parts of you that are still locked in fear and need to be transformed or transcended.

Pay attention to words, numbers, animals or images that keep repeating themselves.

Because I believe we live in an ordered, loving Universe – not a random one – that is in constant communication with us, I therefore see these recurring patterns as messages to help me on my spiritual journey. They serve a purpose.

If this is happening to you, then consider: What were you thinking when you saw them? What do they mean to you? If you don't know, research them, and find their spiritual significance. Examine the feelings they evoke. Record those insights and examine them later. Oftentimes, we don't see the immediate meaning, but with a bit of distance, the meaning will come to us.

Go for a walk in an unfamiliar neighborhood, without plans or lists.

Obviously, don't put yourself in any physical danger, but do try to get out of your comfort zone and routine. Now, pay attention to your surroundings. Does anything stand out to you? Do your eyes go to a particular sign or object? Do you see, smell, hear or taste something that reminds you of a moment in your life? Follow that feeling.

Check in with your intuition. Does it feel right? Act on

it, even if your mind tells you it is nothing but a silly coincidence. Again, don't put yourself in any danger, but challenge yourself to do this, maintaining an open, curious, playful attitude.

Without this practice of following signs and synchronicities, and listening to my intuition, I never would have made it to Jerusalem. They were my cornerstones for making decisions in daily unknowns, and for trusting the path that was leading me.

The synchronicities and repetitive signs were my outer yellow arrows.

My intuition was my inner yellow arrow.

With practice, you will begin to appreciate that there is a current of love in motion around you at all times, and all you have to do is tune in to it when you feel lost or confused to show you the way.

You will see that the more you flow with this great current, the more that you will receive what you need, when you need it, to make the best decision for you in that moment.

You will know that you are already wise enough, capable enough, magnificent enough, loved enough; and that there is nothing you have to do except embrace that.

The more you do this, the more confident you become in yourself, in your ability to handle whatever comes your way, and to take the next step alone.

This is what it means to walk alone without the safety net of an organized pilgrimage path.

This is what it means to walk alone, but never feel alone.

My daily practice became (and remains) keeping an open heart, and connecting to what I know to be my (and your) essence: Love. I do this through yoga, meditation, breathing exercises and surrounding myself with positive people. I limit how much news I watch, and seek the change-makers and builders in difficult situations. These steps help me remain connected to Source – to Love – so that I may perceive its guidance in my Life and act from a place of greater wisdom and power.

Long before I took my first steps as a pilgrim, I became aware of signs as confirmations of decisions I was making. I was becoming more confident in my ability to interpret what was happening, and trusting my intuition a lot more.

When I finally quit my job, the signs intensified. I remember the day I was cleaning out my office, and feeling both excited and nervous because I had no idea what I would be doing next. My phone rang, and it was a friend inviting me to attend a workshop dedicated to helping people discover the life purpose. The creators of this technique, the Walkers, traveled extensively with their seminar schedule but, due to a misprint on their brochure, were unexpectedly in town, holding a session that weekend in a location that was a mere two-hour drive from my home. When I called, they had one final spot available.

I registered without hesitation, believing all this to be a sign. What emerged at the end of this intense process was the picture of a woman who desperately craved peace and who wanted to dedicate her life to it.

The Walkers commented that not only did my entire face light up when I spoke about peace, but an area appeared on my forehead that was lighter than the rest of my face and shaped like a six-sided star. More curiously, they also heard an eagle's call while I spoke, which they admitted was a rare occurrence. They knew that an eagle lived in the mountains nearby, but had only ever seen it once before. They took this as an important omen, an invitation for me to accept the eagle as my totem, or power animal, and my guide in the next stages of my life.

I found it all intriguing, but resisted accepting a totem as powerful as the eagle, which I knew to be the symbol of spiritual vision and reaching for higher realms. After all, I reasoned, who am I?

During one of our breaks, to my great amazement, I saw an eagle flying past, gliding low over the waters, its majestic wings cutting through the air, slowly, powerfully, and eventually disappearing over the mountainous horizon. In those eternal seconds, I was speechless. Was this a sign? Was the eagle speaking with me directly?

I eventually convinced myself that no, the eagle had not come to me personally and that this sighting was nothing more than a happy coincidence…until I returned to the same location two months later. To my astonishment, the same eagle landed a few short meters ahead of me and stared directly into my eyes, as if defying me to ignore his call. This time, I couldn't.

That incident would cement my relationship with the eagle and six-sided star. Any time I saw them – as images or words, spray-painted on a wall, on a billboard, discarded piece of paper, etc. – I stopped and paid attention to what was happening around me. Combined with other signs, these messengers of the Divine would bring me to the people and experiences that would facilitate my journeys and make them into deeply transformational ones.

PUTTING IT ALL TOGETHER

7 PUTTING IT ALL TOGETHER

You've prepared as best as you can. You've begun the practice of expanding your perspectives, and how you see and interpret the world. You feel ready on all levels, ready to take the first steps of your pilgrimage alone.

Let's put it all together.

Let Go of your Plans

At the beginning of this book, I suggested that you research and plan your pilgrimage. Now that you've done it and your mind is at ease, it's time to set those plans aside so that you can begin to listen to your own inner guidance.

As uncomfortable as it many feel in the beginning, letting go is the key to a journey filled with magic and wonder. All manner of events can unfold that are well beyond your ability to control or plan for.

Allow the Path to guide you, to carry you.

Trust that you will know how to handle a situation if or when it arises. Believe in yourself.

Trust in others, in life and in the path that you are walking.

Do you know what we did during our walk to Jerusalem when we had no idea which path to take and no clear sign showed the way? We asked to walk the path of our highest good and the highest good of all... and flipped a coin. We then walked that path with determination, never looking back.

Be Present

Pay attention to what is happening around you, to the people you meet, the conversations you have. They are there by design, not by chance.

There are no coincidences when you are on pilgrimage and walking with an open heart and curious mind. All interactions have meaning. All serve your emotional, mental and spiritual growth.

Take note of how you feel; of the thoughts and memories these interactions evoke.

Pay attention to what is happening within you. Respect whatever you are feeling, and allow it to move through you.

Remember, pilgrimage is an opportunity to explore and make peace with whatever has tormented you. What is buried often comes up during pilgrimage, and can take you by surprise. Examine it. Give thanks for it for this great gift of healing being offered you by a path and universe that deeply loves you.

Lay down your Burdens

As much as you have prepared, there will still be invisible weight that you carry: pain, trauma, grief. Experience has shown me that these often weigh us down, and slow us down, more any physical weight we may carry.

Pilgrimage is an invitation to lay them down.

On the Camino specifically, there is the tradition of putting your sorrows and pains into a stone that you bring with you from your country or that you pick up along the way; and then leaving the stone at *Cruz de Fero*, in Galicia.

I believe the entire path is sacred, so when you feel ready to lay down those burdens, lay that stone down and ask the Camino to take care of it. Give thanks for the experience, and walk away lighter on all levels.

Repeat this ritual as often as you need.

Be Grateful

Gratitude is perhaps the most powerful tool you have as a pilgrim, and is the secret to transforming any difficulties along the way.

Give thanks for EVERY THING: the sun and the rain,

the cold and the heat, the mountains and the valleys, the company and the solitude.

Give thanks for your struggles – physical, emotional, mental and spiritual – for they are the guardians of a great treasure of wisdom. They are the vehicle through which you are offered the unparalleled opportunity to grow in love, compassion, acceptance and peace.

Always Remember:

The tourist demands.
The pilgrim gives thanks.

Journal
Write, sketch or record everything: dreams, unusual conversations, memories, and anything that evokes a strong feeling.

They may not make sense right away but, after some time and far from pilgrimage, their meaning will become apparent to you.

Keep walking
Rest when you need it, but keep moving forward, one step at a time. You may fall behind other pilgrims or veer off the path, but all is well. It is your path, and the one you need to walk. All of it serves your inner journey.

If that means you need to take a taxi to next stop, or that you need to have your backpack shipped ahead, or that you need to sleep in private accommodations, then do so! You are still a pilgrim, as authentic as any other.

Have Fun!
You're on a great adventure, meeting people from around the world, exploring a new culture and growing in ways you never could have anticipated. It's impossible not to be enriched by this experience. It will leave a smile on your face long after you leave it. So have fun with it. Walk

lightly and with great joy, knowing that you are supported and are walking towards what is perhaps the most sacred of all destinations: your radiant, eternal, self!

A PILGRIM IN THE WORLD:
A WAY OF BEING

8 A PILGRIM IN THE WORLD: A WAY OF BEING

What you have hopefully gleaned from these pages is that by preparing the mental, emotional and spiritual elements of your pilgrimage, you now walk the path with greater confidence, feeling aligned on all levels.

For many pilgrims, the journey ends as soon as they arrive at the sacred destination. They feel elated, powerful, grateful, joyful, brilliant, and want to hold on to those feelings; but in the crush of their everyday lives, find it difficult to do so. They feel adrift, unable to focus, lacking a passion for their work and life that once defined them. Many return to the path over and again trying to recapture those feelings, but again find them elusive upon their return home.

I believe this is because the purpose of pilgrimage has been misunderstood. The path is there for us to strengthen our spirits, to heal what needs to be resolved, to awaken us to our grander selves and to our higher purpose. It is not an escape from our life, but the opportunity to stand more confidently in our unique light so that we may share it more powerfully wherever we are.

This is why pilgrims who have finished their pilgrimages are called stars – *estrellas*!

It is upon your return home that your true life journey – your life as a pilgrim in the world – begins.

How to Ease the Transition
Like all great journeys, you need time to digest all that has happened to you and begin to integrate the lessons you have learned into your everyday life. That can't happen if you immerse yourself too quickly into your life and work.

If you can, give yourself at least a week at the end of your pilgrimage to begin the process of re-integration. Read your diaries. Meditate. Try to weave a thread that links your experiences, encounters, dreams, conversations into a coherent whole, into a message that your soul (or wisest part of you) is bringing you, offering clarity and direction for your life now.

Alberto and I needed over a year to go through our diaries and truly assimilate what had happened to us during those thirteen months of pilgrimage. We read through our diaries, relived some of the more profound experiences (including the arguments!), made notes about what they were truly teaching us. They became the foundation not only for our book, but for how we would choose to live our lives moving forward. We decided not go back to the corporate world from whence we both came, and to dedicate our lives to sharing with others the perspective and consciousness that our pilgrimages offered us.

We also committed ourselves to continuing our spiritual, emotional and mental journey in the world: that journey of growth and transformation didn't end in Santiago de Compostela or Jerusalem, and continues to this day. In essence, we are pilgrims in our everyday life.

Speaking with other pilgrims, especially those of like mind and heart, can be helpful as family and friends often tire of yet one more pilgrimage story!

In continually reliving our experiences, however, I do believe we risk never moving forward in our lives. The goal of pilgrimage is to give you clarity about your life and the courage to make the necessary changes…not to run away from your life.

So, by all means, share your journey but use its lessons and insights to make the long-lasting changes you need in order to feel the same joy, simplicity and openness you felt during pilgrimage.

Continue to connect with nature, and to walk in the unhurried pace of the pilgrim.

Practice being present to all that is occurring around

you and within you. Pay attention to the sounds, the scents, the sights. Take them all in, and feel your connection to them. It is here, in this feeling of oneness with all of existence, that the miracle and mystery of life exists. It is in this place that all is possible. Give thanks for the fact that you are here to experience it all and for the journey that has brought you here.

Try to see the people in your life as pilgrims on their own journeys of life, partners on this great pilgrimage that is Life. Try to understand them, to see them beyond the labels or job positions or masks or routines… try to see the soul that is in front of you. To see the divine spark in them, just as it is in you.

Try to see this spark in all living things, animals, plants, because it is already there!

Find moments of stillness, whether it's during a walk or in meditation or simply sitting by yourself. In that place of quiet, open yourself to receive guidance for the next step in your journey. The same Love that walked with you on your pilgrimage is with you now, and always. Connect with it. Feel it. Feel its warmth. Feel its pride in you, its deep love for you.

From that place of feeling loved, all our troubles dissolve and we make room for new thoughts to enter. We are able to see possibilities when perhaps none existed before.

Ask to be shown the next step in your life, one that will allow you to be free, joyful, trusting, fulfilled.

Then, just as in pilgrimage, take that one step in the direction of what inspires or calls you, knowing that the next step will reveal itself to you and you will know how to take it.

You don't see the whole road ahead of you when you walk, so why do you need to see the whole roadmap of your life? Can you not walk it metaphorically in the way of the pilgrim?

Continue exploring aspects of yourself that emerged during pilgrimage, and expand on them.

Perhaps you discovered an interest in architecture. Or storytelling. Or healing. Or ministry. Or counseling. Or painting. Or writing. Or a myriad of other possibilities that emerged during pilgrimage. They are important aspects of who you truly are, aspects that perhaps had been too long buried and finally given free reign (perhaps even permission) during your pilgrimage.

If they make your heart come alive, then pursue them.

PILGRIMAGES BEYOND SPAIN

9 PILGRIMAGES BEYOND SPAIN

More and more, pilgrims are looking for routes that lead them to sacred locations around the world. For the most part, they are not as well organized and structured as the Camino.

The paths are being studied and marked by various local associations passionate about identifying and preserving the original routes as walked by pilgrims through their countries. The infrastructure is being built. The signs are being painted. Some of these routes are connecting to the Silk Road, which is also being marked.

Here are some of the international routes being considered. Map courtesy of Giovanni Caselli.

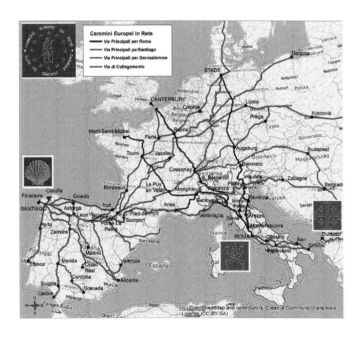

What you Need to Know

There are no albergues run by municipalities or donation-based accommodations. They are private, so you will need to research and book them in advance.

Reach out to the various groups and associations taking on the task of marking these routes. A list follows. Many have both websites and Facebook pages, and are run by pilgrim volunteers who are more than eager to share their knowledge. I encourage you to join their mailing lists and groups, and get in touch with them directly. The "Confraternity of Pilgrims to Jerusalem" is an excellent Facebook resource for pilgrims walking to Jerusalem.

If you weren't resilient before, this type of unstructured pilgrimage will either develop it in you or break you. Now more than ever, you must be willing to let go of your plans and flow with the circumstances and experiences that present themselves to you.

Make sure you have the proper visas for the countries you are walking through. Often, you can buy them right at the border you are crossing on foot, but it is better to know this information beforehand and to know how many days you are allowed to legally stay in that country.

As a precaution, advise your embassy in that country of your whereabouts.

In many countries, you are walking through towns and villages where credit cards are not accepted, and bank machines may only be found in the larger cities. Be sure to carry cash in the local currency. I normally didn't carry more than the equivalent of $100USD, and stocked up as needed in the larger cities. Prices for common goods vary in each country, so the amount you spend will differ. For this reason, it is difficult to create a budget. I was out of my country on travel and pilgrimage for 24 months. During that time, I estimate that I spent about $10,000USD for hotels, meals, buses, ferries. That doesn't include my flights to and from Canada to Europe. Keep in mind that for the first six months of my pilgrimage to Jerusalem, we were calling on churches for shelter. It was from Greece onwards that we began paying for hostels.

If you are a woman walking alone, it is imperative that you follow the cultural and religious norms of the country you're walking through. In more conservative countries, wear clothing that covers your arms and legs. Carry or buy a headscarf. It is required to enter mosques, some churches and other spiritual centers.

I would encourage you to know a few words in the language of the country you're walking through. Knowing how to say basic greetings often carries more weight than any currency you may have in your pocket.

You are often relying on the kindness of strangers to help you, so walking with an open, curious and respectful attitude is more important than ever.

If you have a tent, be sure to ask the permission of the landowner whose land you plan on using for the evening.
If you don't have a tent and there are no hotels or hostels in the town, go to the local church, monastery, convent or spiritual center and ask to sleep in the church hall or any place they have where you can lay out your sleeping bag.

Explain that you are a pilgrim; that you have money and food, that you only need shelter from the elements for one night, and that you will continue on your way the next day.

Offer to work for your stay, if necessary.

Local bartenders are an invaluable source of information, especially in the smaller towns and villages. Ask their help in finding accommodations for the night.

I carried detailed maps of each region I was walking in, and bought them as soon as I entered the area. I did not buy them in advance, and cut out any extraneous parts that were not part of my route. You may want to consider using GPS, as many associations now have GPS markers for their paths.

You can buy what you need along the way. I didn't expect my pilgrimage to last a year, and had mostly fall-winter clothing. In the summer, I shipped my heavy items home and bought light clothing as needed. When the weather cooled again in November-December, I bought a light jacket. You can try to plan for, and carry, all your gear but weather is the most unpredictable of elements in your journey.

Marked Routes
- ❖ Via Francigena (aka Via London to Rome) from Canterbury, UK to Rome, Italy.
  http://www.viefrancigene.org/en/

- ❖ Via Engatia from Durres, Albania to Istanbul, Turkey.
  http://www.viaegnatiafoundation.eu/index.php/hiking-wandern/via-egnatia-hiking-trail

- ❖ Via Postumia from Aquilea to Genova, Italy.
  https://en.wikipedia.org/wiki/Via_Postumia

- ❖ Cammino di Assisi, Path of St. Francis of Assisi.
  http://www.camminodiassisi.it/EN/

- ❖ St. Olav's Way or the Old Kings' Road are six

pilgrimage routes, all leading to the Nidaros Cathedral in Trondheim, Norway, site of the tomb of St. Olav. http://pilegrimsleden.no/en/

❖ Via Romea Germanica from Stade, Germany to Rome, Italy. http://www.viaromeagermanica.com/

❖ Shikoku pilgrimage of 88 Temples in Japan. http://www.shikokuhenrotrail.com/.

International Pilgrims
❖ Giovanni Caselli is probably THE noted international pilgrimage scholar and researcher. His Facebook page "Global Network of Ancient Ways" is a treasure trove of information, as is Giovanni himself. https://www.facebook.com/globalnetworkpeace/

❖ Peace Pilgrim walked over 25,000 miles on a personal pilgrimage for peace all over North America with nothing but a pen, comb, toothbrush and map. http://www.peacepilgrim.org/.

❖ Thair Abud walked from Graz, Austria to Mecca. http://onthewaytoday.wordpress.com.

❖ Party Pilgrims are a couple who walked from Canterbury, England to Jerusalem. http://partypilgrims.com/Party_Pilgrims/Home.html

❖ Brandon Wilson walked from Dijon, France to Jerusalem, following a route called the Templar Trail that Godfrey de Bouillon and his army traveled in 1096 to Jerusalem. http://www.pilgrimstales.com/about_brandonwilson. html

❖ Jerusalem Way trio of pilgrims walked from Austria to

Jerusalem. http://www.jerusalemway.org/

❖ Winter Pilgrim Ann Sieben is a remarkable woman who has walked alone to many places around the world. http://winterpilgrim.blogspot.ca/

❖ Petr Hirsch walked from his home in the Czech Republic to Santiago, then the Iberian Peninsula back to Rome and then Jerusalem. http://petr-hirsch.cz/

❖ Sara Zanni walked from Milan, Italy to Santiago. http://www.100daysontheway.com/?p=1117

❖ Out of Eden Walk – Although he visits many sites of pilgrimage, this is journalist Paul Salopek's multiyear, 21,000-mile storytelling odyssey across the globe in the footsteps of our ancestors. http://learn.outofedenwalk.com/.

❖ Tor and Siffy Torkildson have a Facebook group called "The Walkabout Chronicles-Epic Journeys by Foot" with daily examples of people walking and hiking in many remote parts of the world. Some of these places are pilgrimages.

Organized Walks

❖ Jorsala – annual walk for reconciliation and peacebuilding, with varying routes each year. http://www.jorsala.org/

❖ European Peace Walk – annual cultural walk, linking Vienna to Venice. http://www.peacewalk.eu/

❖ Pilgrims Crossing Borders – annual interreligious walk for diversity and dialogue, from Trondheim to Jerusalem. http://picrobo.blogspot.ca/

❖ Pad Yatra, meaning "journey on foot", visits the most sacred sites for Buddhists in southern Nepal and northern India, where it is believed the Buddha lived and taught. http://www.padyatra.org/.

A BLESSING FROM THE PATH

Step lightly and with reverence, for you walk on paths forged by sacrifice, devotion and love. You are not merely stepping onto sacred ground, but into what is sacred within you. Treat both delicately.

Taste of my abundance. Dwell in my magic places. Drink of my beauty. They are all freely shared, and reside within you too.

Leave your sorrows and travails with me, so that the flames of my sword may unleash their hidden light. But don't forget to also leave me your joys and triumphs, for they are my nourishment too.

The sacred in you resides in me also. That is because we are created by the same hand. No separation exists between us. My imprint on your heart is as binding as your imprint on mine.

I speak more to your heart and soul, and less to your mind. I am the worker of miracles. I lead you to the most unexpected places, places that feel both familiar and unrecognizable. I lead you to the greatest treasure, the one that you were carrying with you all along.

~ Mony

ABOUT THE AUTHOR

Mony is a storyteller, inspirational speaker and international award-winning author of "Walking for Peace, an inner journey". Together with Alberto Agraso, her pilgrim husband, they are social entrepreneurs creating books and artwork that transform and empower lives. She is host and producer of "The Author's Journey" on Rogers TV in Canada, and "The Pilgrim Story Hour" video series, sharing stories, tips and lessons learned from her pilgrimages.

Made in the USA
Middletown, DE
15 February 2019